Do Whales Ever...?

Written by Nathalie Ward

Illustrated by Tessa Morgan

Down East Books • Camden, Maine

For my folks, who taught me to dare to ask,
and Aanjes, whose questions make me listen,
wonder, and discover. – N. W.

For my children: Jennifer, Dylan, and Nicholas. –T. M.

Text copyright © 1997 by Nathalie F. R. Ward
Illustrations © 1997 by Tessa Morgan
Layout and typography by Ruth Ann Hill
Printed and bound in Hong Kong
through Oceanic Graphic Printing (USA) Inc.

5   4   3   2

DOWN EAST BOOKS / *Camden, Maine*

LIBRARY OF CONGRESS CATALOGING-IN-PUBLICATION DATA

Ward, Nathalie, 1951–
        Do whales ever--? / Nathalie F. R. Ward ; illustrated by Tessa Morgan
            p.   cm.
        Summary: Answers a variety of questions on the habits and characteristics of whales.
        ISBN 0-89272-368-8
        1. Whales--Juvenile literature. [Whales. 2. Questions and answers.]
    I. Morgan, Tessa. 1959– ill.   II. Title.
    QL737.C4W323   1997
    599.5--dc20   96-11975
                                                                                        CIP
                                                                                        AC

Do Whales Ever...?

Do whales have belly buttons?
Do they ever get fleas?
How do whales hiccup?
Can they possibly sneeze?

What color are whales' eyes?
How big are their ears?
Do they smack their lips?
How far can they hear?

Some questions seem silly,
But others do not.
Do whales ever sweat?
In fact, do they get hot?

Do they get sad?
Do whales ever cry?
What's it like to be wet
And never be dry?

Do whales ever snore?
And how do they sleep?
Can whales taste their food,
Whether salty or sweet?

If they don't clean their teeth
The way you and I do,
Don't they get cavities
And bad toothaches too?

Whales eat fish and squid
And live in the sea,
But what I really want to know
Is . . . do they pee?

Risso's Dolphin

Southern Rightwhale Dolphin

Spinner Dolphin

Introducing—The cetaceans.

"Say what?"

The whales, porpoises, and dolphins. Scientists call all whales cetaceans (*sa-TAY-shuns*).

Just like us, whales are mammals, so they must breathe air. They are warm-blooded. Whale babies are born alive instead of hatched from eggs, and they drink milk from their mother.

Orcas

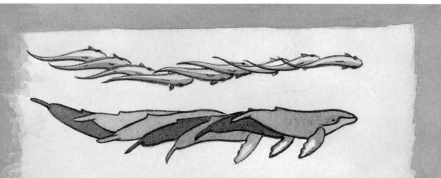

At first glance, whales seem to look like fish—but look closely at their tails. Fish move their tails from side to side as they swim. Whales' tails move up and down.

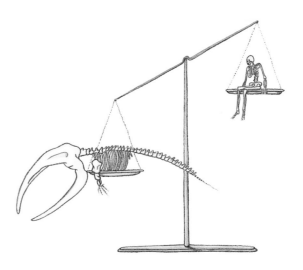

Did whales ever have legs?

The ancestors of whales lived on land, millions of years ago, and they did have legs. Today's whales have evolved to live only under water, so their front limbs have become flippers and their hind limbs have disappeared—almost. Deep inside the muscles near the tail flukes are two tiny bones that are not even connected to the rest of the whale's skeleton. These bones are all that is left of a whale's legs.

The rest of a whale's skeleton can be huge. A human skeleton weighs about 25 pounds, but a humpback whale's skeleton can weigh more than 20,000 pounds—that's as heavy as a small cruise ship.

It is possible for whale's bones to break. Scientists have found broken ribs and flippers in some whale skeletons.

Little Giants

A large whale, like the Brydes (*BRY-dees*) whale is pregnant for almost 12 months. At birth, the calf may be 14 feet long and weigh almost a ton. That's about the weight of a small pickup truck.

A 20-foot newborn blue whale is even bigger. Its mother's milk is very rich and looks like cottage cheese. A hungry blue whale calf drinks as much as 84 gallons of milk a day. It may gain an amazing 9 pounds an hour, and it can grow more than an inch a day.

A mother pilot whale will nurse her calf for more than two years. Most whales will nurse for one year.

Twin calves are rare. They probably don't survive because the mother would have a hard time supplying enough milk.

Do whales have belly buttons?

Just like other mammals, whales do have belly buttons where their umbilical cord used to be.

Whales are born tail-first. A newborn whale's fins, flippers, and flukes are very rubbery and soft. After birth, the mother twists and turns to break the umbilical cord. Then she nudges her calf to the surface to take its first breath.

Within the first week, the calf's cord withers away and drops off, and a belly button is left behind.

1

2

3

Pilot Whale

4

Skin Deep

A whale's body is covered with rubberlike skin. Most whales have back fins, called dorsal fins. All whales have flippers. The flippers look like smooth, rounded paddles. But check out what's inside: the bones look like your finger bones.

Whale   **Human**

Whales' tails, called flukes, do not have any bones. They are made of cartilage, which is almost as strong as steel. Your nose is made of the same material.

beluga

humpback

sperm whale

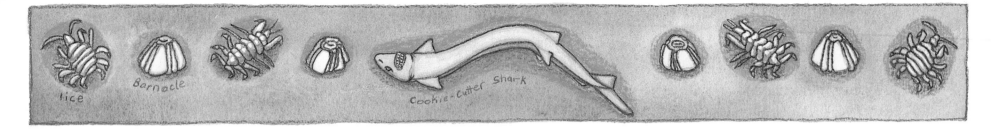

lice
Barnacle
Cookie-Cutter Shark

Do whales get fleas?

Whales don't get fleas, but they do have other hitch-hikers that can be quite a nuisance. What do these unwelcome guests look like?

Whale lice look like tiny crabs, about the size of a button. They crawl into the creases and folds on right whales' heads.

Barnacles can be pests, too. They cement their hard shells onto a whale's skin. Barnacles can be as small as a fingernail or as large as a fist. One humpback whale was found with more than half a ton of barnacles on its body—that's two pickup trucks full.

Cookie-cutter sharks also damage whales' skin. They hang onto whales and dolphins by using their lips as suction pads. Then they scoop out a circle of flesh with their razor-sharp teeth. The inch-deep hole leaves a two-inch round scar on the whale.

Right Whale

"Blows! Blows!"
they shout, when they see the whale spout.

A whale's breath, or blow, looks like a spout of water or a puff of steam. Although whales live in water, they always return to the surface to fill their lungs with air. A whale's nostril is called a blowhole. It is on top of its head.

Gray Whale

Bottlenose dolphins can hold their breath for five minutes. Sperm whales are the champion divers—they can hold their breath for more than one and a half hours. A sperm whale takes two breaths in a minute. How many times do you breathe in a minute?

Do whales ever hiccup?

Because they breathe air like humans, whales have lungs and a diaphragm (*DIE-a-fram*). The diaphragm is a flat, strong membrane that looks like thin rubber. It separates the lungs from the stomach and other organs. (Place your hands on your bottom rib and watch your stomach move in and out as you breathe. That's where your diaphragm is located.)

Every once in a while, the diaphragm jerks suddenly, causing a sharp *hiccup* sound. It seems possible that whales can hiccup, too, though nobody has yet heard that happen!

A Tooth Is a Tooth Is a Tooth

There are two groups of whales: the toothed whales and the baleen (*bay-LEAN*) whales. Toothed whales feed mostly on fish and squid. Most toothed whales, such as porpoises and dolphins, are smaller than the large baleen whales. But watch out! A sperm whale may be the size of your school bus—almost 60 feet long—and weigh as much as 50 tons!

Teeth come in weird sizes and shapes. Sperm whales have about 50 fist-sized teeth in their lower jaw. A bottlenose dolphin has as many as 100 sharp little teeth. Some beaked whales have only 2 teeth. A narwhal's tooth, or tusk, may be as long as 6 feet.

Strap-toothed Whale

Narwhal

Blainville's Beaked Whale

Do whales ever get cavities?

Whale's teeth are made out of the same materials as our teeth—dentine and enamel. Sometimes food particles get trapped in the spaces between their teeth and cause decay.

Scientists have found blackened teeth in some sperm whales, so whales can get cavities and probably toothaches too. And if a whale loses a tooth, it doesn't grow back.

Sperm Whale

Open Wide—
Let's See What's Inside

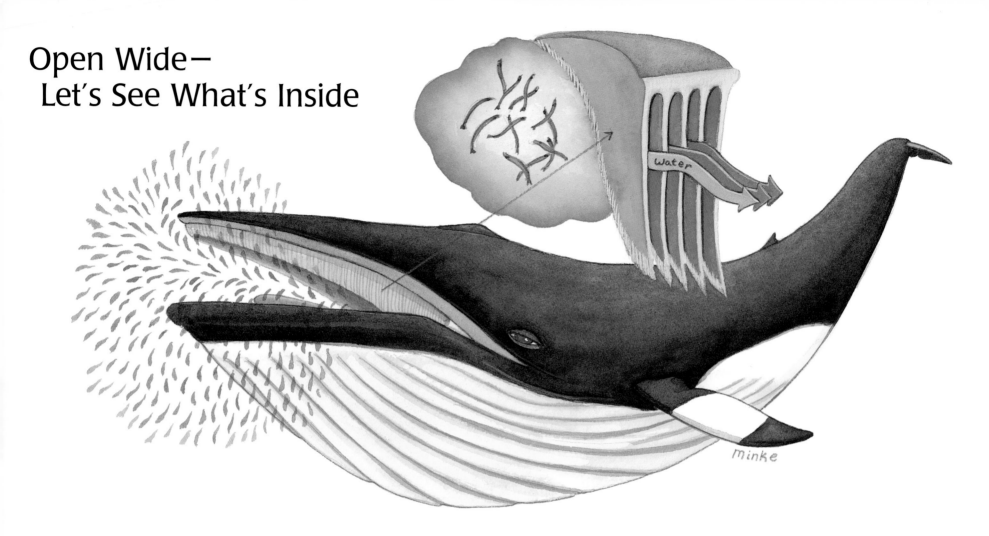

Baleen whales, like the minke (*MING-key*) whale, do not have teeth. Instead, hundreds of strands hang down from their upper jaw like the teeth on a comb. These are called baleen plates.

Some species of baleen whales eat small fish. Others eat tiny creatures, called plankton, that drift on or near the surface of the water. The baleen acts like a giant strainer. First the whale scoops up a huge mouthful of water. Then it lets the water pour out through the gaps in the baleen, leaving behind a mouthful of plankton or wriggling fish.

Do whales go to the bathroom?

A bottlenose dolphin eats 25 pounds of fish a day. A sei (*say*) whale may eat 150 pounds in one gulp. Most whales have three stomachs to help them digest all that food. And as everyone knows, what goes in must come out. Whale waste comes out as clear urine and as a brown powder that dissolves quickly in the water.

You may wonder whether whales drink salt water. All animals, including whales, must have fresh water to live. Whales obtain fresh water from the plankton and fish that they eat. Whales' kidneys remove the excess salt from their blood.

The northern right whale eats more than four tons of plankton a day—that's equal to 8000 boxes of spaghetti.

"Pass the plankton, please!"

Bounce Me Now

When you throw a ball against a wall, it bounces back to you. Dolphins and other toothed whales send and receive sounds in the same way. They find food by sending out clicking sounds, which bounce off objects such as a school of fish. Then dolphins listen for the echo that bounces back. The echo tells the dolphin what they have found and how far away it is. This process is called echolocation.

Sound travels faster and farther under water than it does in air. Some whales can hear sounds from more than 50 miles away. Like elephants, whales can hear much lower-pitched and higher-pitched sounds than humans can.

Common Dolphin

Do whales have ears?

A whale's ears are tiny openings—about the width of a pencil. They are found behind the whale's eyes. A long canal stretches from the outer ear hole to the inner ear. The canal is filled with a wax plug that keeps water from getting inside.

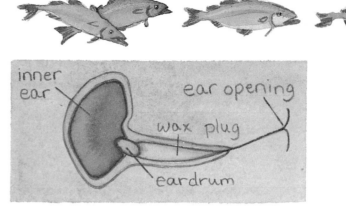

inner ear · ear opening · wax plug · eardrum

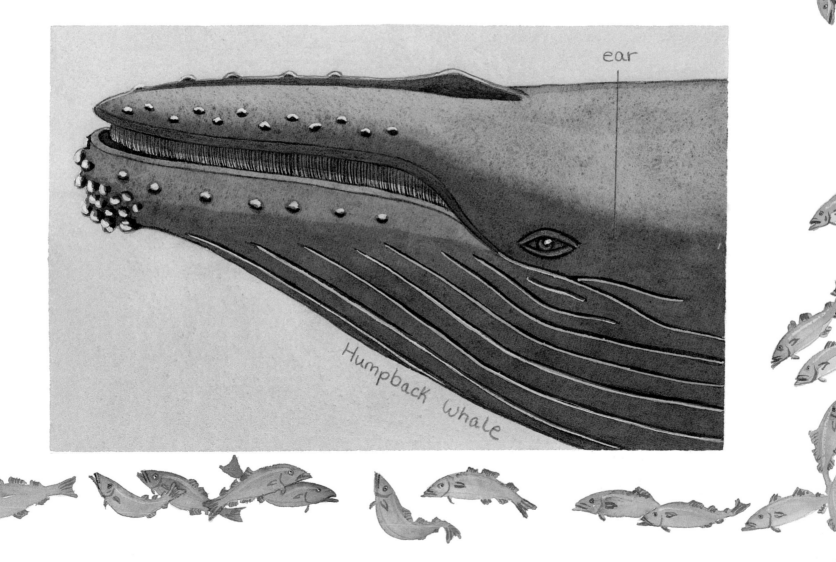

ear

Humpback Whale

Fast Foods—Let's Eat

   Toothed whales use special organs in their rounded heads to find food by echolocation. Baleen whales can't do this, so how do they find *their* food? Perhaps baleen whales use different senses. Since they don't smell very well, they may find fish by sight or hearing.

Blue Whale

Do whales ever smack their lips?

Whales don't chew their food, so they probably don't smack. They do snap their jaws together when they are annoyed, making a loud, explosive sound.

Since whales swallow their food whole, they probably don't need to taste their food. Perhaps that's why all sorts of strange objects have been found in their stomachs—such as feathers, balloons, and even a bouquet of flowers. A whale's tongue has very few taste buds, so they probably taste very little.

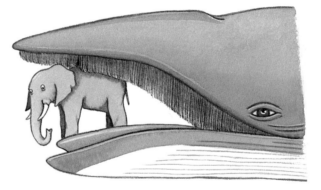

How Big Is a Big Tongue?

A blue whale's tongue is huge. It is about 15 feet long and weighs about four tons. That's the same weight as an elephant. Because its tongue is attached to the bottom of its mouth, a whale could not touch its tongue to its nose—even if it *had* a nose.

Oooh–
What lovely lips you have, and those eyes . . .

Whales can see above and below the water. The position of their eyes and the shape of their head affects how a whale or a dolphin sees. A dolphin can see straight ahead as well as to the side. A sperm whale's eyes are so far apart that it has a blind spot in front.

Do whales ever have green eyes?

At birth, some whales have *blue* eyes, but all adults have brown eyes.

When a whale lifts its head above water, or spyhops, it is checking you out. How well can whales see? Scientists think whales can see colors. Because they often live in murky water, they probably can see things close up but not far away.

Blind as a Bat?

Not all cetaceans live in salt water. Some are found in the muddiest rivers in the world. Boto dolphins, which live in the Amazon River, have the smallest eyes of any cetacean—so tiny that these pink dolphins are almost blind. They use echolocation to hunt and find food, just as bats do on land.

All river dolphins have long beaks, many pointed teeth, and a strange habit of swimming on their sides or upside down.

Boto Dolphin

Do whales ever cry?

Have you ever opened your eyes underwater? They sting a little, especially in salt water. Whales have special oily tears that constantly bathe their eyes. This oil protects the eyes from stinging in salty or muddy water.

Like us, whales have eyelids, so they can blink, but they don't have eyelashes to help keep dirt out of their eyes.

Blubber Makes the Whale Grow Round

All whales have a layer of fat, called blubber, underneath their skin. Most dolphins and porpoises have a blubber layer about half an inch thick. The blubber of a bowhead whale may be an amazing 20 inches thick.

Blubber acts like a storehouse for energy. When there is no food, the whale's body uses this fat as a fuel. Can you guess what else blubber does?

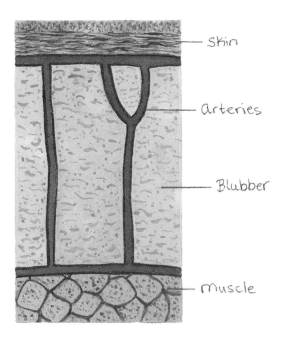

Skin

Arteries

Blubber

Muscle

Narwhal

Do whales ever freeze in cold water?

Unlike most mammals, cetaceans do not have thick coats of hair to keep them warm. Even so, many whales—such as the beluga whale, the narwhal, and the bowhead whale—live in water that is covered with ice most of the year. Their blubber works like an overcoat to keep body heat in so the whales stay warm.

Sometimes whales face the opposite problem: how to cool off. Whales have no pores on their skin, or sweat glands, so they can't perspire. To cool down, a whale's body increases blood flow to the dorsal fin, flippers, and flukes, which act like radiators to dump heat.

Dall's Porpoise

Right whale

Bowhead whale

Beluga

Growing Up

A sperm whale calf may nurse for up to ten years. After the young whale begins to find food on its own, it takes another ten years before the whale is mature and looks for a mate. An adult sperm whale may live to be 60 years old. A harbor porpoise may only live to about 17 years of age.

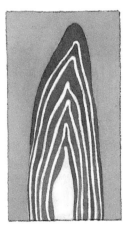

To find out how old a whale is, scientists slice a tooth in half to count the rings. A whale's tooth grows in layers like a tree. Each pair of rings—one light and one dark—equals one year. How old is this whale?

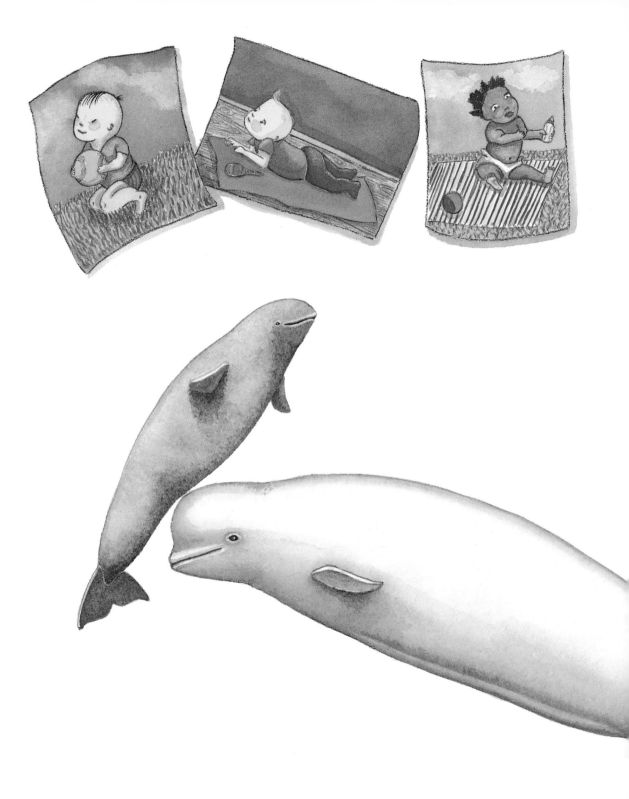

Do whales change as they grow older?

Most baby whales look like smaller versions of their parents. But some species are a different color or shape when they are born.

Newborn beluga whales are gray but gradually turn white as they grow up. The spotted dolphin is born without spots. As it grows older, spots appear first on its head and belly and then all over its body. At birth, a baby Atlantic humpback dolphin looks like any dolphin. But as an adult, it grows a camel-like hump in the middle of its back.

Atlantic Hump-backed Dolphin

Beluga

Spotted Dolphin

Sea Tunes

Whales are chatterboxes. Bottlenose dolphins chirp and whistle to each other. Sperm whales make loud clicking sounds. Finback whales rumble and groan. Beluga whales squeal and moo.

These sounds have special meanings. Whales may "talk" to help keep a family group together, to warn others of danger or to call for help, and even to discuss lunch plans.

Do whales really sing?

If you could dive into the water near a humpback whale, you would discover a whole world of humpback whale sounds.

> *Whoo-oo-op yup.*
> *Eee oooh ahh.*
> *Eee yup yup.*

These groans, moans, and squeaks are just some of the sounds made by a singing male humpback whale. A whale song is a repeated pattern of sound that may last thirty minutes. Scientists think that males try to attract a female with this underwater tune. Males sing at any time of day and night, but mostly during the winter, when they are in the warm waters of their breeding grounds.

ZZZZZ-zzzzzzzz

Sometimes a whale swims very slowly or lies motionless just beneath the surface. It looks like a floating log.

Do whales ever sleep?

Whales and dolphins have a special way of resting. They "sleep" with one half of their brain at a time. Scientists believe that while one half of their brain rests, the other stays "awake" and alerts the dolphin to breathe and swim. The brain halves take turns resting.

Do you think whales snore? It might be possible for them to snore, but we still do not know the answer.

Shhh-hhh-hhh–it may be sleeping.

The Tail End

Children often ask questions that adults don't dare to ask. When my daughter was five years old, she asked, "Do whales ever have fleas?"

I heard even more questions when I worked as a naturalist on whalewatch boats. It was my job to tell people about whales. I always enjoyed the kids' curiosity. They wanted to know all sorts of things: Do whales get wrinkles? Do whales drink salt water? Do they get stomach aches? Are they ticklish?

I wrote *Do Whales Ever . . . ?* to answer some of these great questions.

Nathalie Ward